35 Egg-Free Baking Recipes for Home

By: Kelly Johnson

Table of Contents

- Chocolate Chip Cookies
- Banana Bread
- Vegan Brownies
- Blueberry Muffins
- Pumpkin Pie
- Oatmeal Raisin Cookies
- Lemon Drizzle Cake
- Coconut Macaroons
- Raspberry Crumble Bars
- Carrot Cake
- Peanut Butter Cookies
- Zucchini Bread
- Snickerdoodles
- Apple Crisp
- Almond Butter Blondies
- Red Velvet Cupcakes
- Gingerbread Cookies
- Strawberry Shortcake
- Pineapple Upside-Down Cake
- Cinnamon Rolls
- Chocolate Cake
- Key Lime Pie
- Peanut Butter Banana Bread
- Black Forest Cake
- Lemon Poppy Seed Muffins
- Sugar Cookies
- Coffee Cake
- Almond Joy Bars
- Raspberry Chocolate Tart
- Pistachio Baklava
- Churros
- Marble Pound Cake
- Oreo Cheesecake
- Salted Caramel Brownies
- Cherry Pie

- Almond Biscotti
- Fig Newtons
- Scones
- Coconut Cream Pie
- Vanilla Cupcakes
- Chocolate Babka
- Pumpkin Roll
- Mocha Cake
- Lemon Bars
- Peanut Butter Fudge
- Caramel Apple Crisp
- Blueberry Cobbler
- Strawberry Rhubarb Crisp
- Maple Pecan Pie
- Molten Lava Cake

Chocolate Chip Cookies

Ingredients:

2 1/4 cups all-purpose flour
1 teaspoon baking soda
1/2 teaspoon salt
1 cup unsalted butter, softened
3/4 cup granulated sugar
3/4 cup packed brown sugar
1 teaspoon vanilla extract
2 cups semisweet chocolate chips

Instructions:

Preheat your oven to 375°F (190°C). Line baking sheets with parchment paper.
In a small bowl, whisk together the flour, baking soda, and salt. Set aside.
In a large mixing bowl, beat together the softened butter, granulated sugar, brown sugar, and vanilla extract until creamy and well combined.
Gradually add the dry ingredients to the wet ingredients, mixing until a dough forms.
Stir in the chocolate chips until evenly distributed throughout the dough.
Using a spoon or cookie scoop, drop rounded tablespoons of dough onto the prepared baking sheets, leaving some space between each cookie.
Bake in the preheated oven for 9 to 11 minutes, or until the cookies are golden brown around the edges.
Allow the cookies to cool on the baking sheets for a few minutes before transferring them to wire racks to cool completely.
Enjoy your delicious egg-free chocolate chip cookies!

Banana Bread

Ingredients:

- 2 cups all-purpose flour
- 1 teaspoon baking soda
- 1/4 teaspoon salt
- 1/2 cup unsalted butter, softened
- 1 cup granulated sugar
- 2 ripe bananas, mashed
- 1/4 cup milk (dairy or non-dairy)
- 1 teaspoon vanilla extract
- Optional: 1/2 cup chopped nuts (such as walnuts or pecans)

Instructions:

Preheat your oven to 350°F (175°C). Grease a 9x5 inch loaf pan or line it with parchment paper.

In a medium bowl, whisk together the flour, baking soda, and salt. Set aside.

In a large mixing bowl, cream together the softened butter and granulated sugar until light and fluffy.

Add the mashed bananas, milk, and vanilla extract to the butter-sugar mixture, and mix until well combined.

Gradually add the dry ingredients to the wet ingredients, mixing until just combined. Be careful not to overmix.

If using nuts, gently fold them into the batter.

Pour the batter into the prepared loaf pan, spreading it out evenly.

Bake in the preheated oven for 60 to 70 minutes, or until a toothpick inserted into the center comes out clean.

Allow the banana bread to cool in the pan for about 10 minutes, then transfer it to a wire rack to cool completely before slicing.

Slice and serve your delicious egg-free banana bread!

Vegan Brownies

Ingredients:

- 1 cup all-purpose flour
- 1/2 cup unsweetened cocoa powder
- 1 teaspoon baking powder
- 1/4 teaspoon salt
- 1 cup granulated sugar
- 1/2 cup unsweetened applesauce
- 1/4 cup vegetable oil
- 1/4 cup almond milk (or any other plant-based milk)
- 1 teaspoon vanilla extract
- 1/2 cup dairy-free chocolate chips (optional)

Instructions:

Preheat your oven to 350°F (175°C). Grease an 8x8 inch baking pan or line it with parchment paper.

In a medium bowl, whisk together the flour, cocoa powder, baking powder, and salt. Set aside.

In a large mixing bowl, combine the granulated sugar, applesauce, vegetable oil, almond milk, and vanilla extract. Mix until well combined.

Gradually add the dry ingredients to the wet ingredients, stirring until just combined. Be careful not to overmix.

If using chocolate chips, fold them into the batter.

Pour the batter into the prepared baking pan, spreading it out evenly.

Bake in the preheated oven for 25 to 30 minutes, or until a toothpick inserted into the center comes out with a few moist crumbs.

Allow the brownies to cool in the pan for about 10 minutes, then transfer them to a wire rack to cool completely before slicing.

Slice and enjoy your delicious vegan brownies!

Blueberry Muffins

Ingredients:

- 1 1/2 cups all-purpose flour
- 1/2 cup granulated sugar
- 2 teaspoons baking powder
- 1/4 teaspoon salt
- 1/3 cup vegetable oil
- 1/2 cup almond milk (or any other plant-based milk)
- 1 teaspoon vanilla extract
- 1 cup fresh or frozen blueberries

Instructions:

Preheat your oven to 375°F (190°C). Line a muffin tin with paper liners or grease the cups lightly.

In a large mixing bowl, whisk together the flour, sugar, baking powder, and salt until well combined.

In a separate bowl, combine the vegetable oil, almond milk, and vanilla extract. Mix well.

Pour the wet ingredients into the dry ingredients and stir until just combined. Do not overmix; a few lumps are fine.

Gently fold in the blueberries until evenly distributed throughout the batter.

Spoon the batter into the prepared muffin cups, filling each about two-thirds full.

Bake in the preheated oven for 18 to 20 minutes, or until a toothpick inserted into the center comes out clean.

Allow the muffins to cool in the tin for a few minutes, then transfer them to a wire rack to cool completely.

Enjoy your egg-free blueberry muffins!

Pumpkin Pie

Ingredients:

For the crust:

- 1 1/4 cups all-purpose flour
- 1/2 teaspoon salt
- 1/2 cup vegetable shortening or vegan butter, cold
- 3-4 tablespoons ice water

For the filling:

- 1 can (15 ounces) pumpkin puree
- 3/4 cup full-fat coconut milk
- 1/2 cup packed brown sugar
- 1/4 cup cornstarch
- 1 teaspoon vanilla extract
- 1 1/2 teaspoons ground cinnamon
- 1/2 teaspoon ground ginger
- 1/4 teaspoon ground nutmeg
- 1/4 teaspoon ground cloves
- 1/4 teaspoon salt

Instructions:

Preheat your oven to 375°F (190°C).

To make the crust, in a large mixing bowl, combine the flour and salt. Cut in the cold vegetable shortening or vegan butter using a pastry cutter or fork until the mixture resembles coarse crumbs.

Gradually add the ice water, 1 tablespoon at a time, mixing with a fork until the dough comes together. Be careful not to overwork the dough.

Shape the dough into a disk, wrap it in plastic wrap, and refrigerate for at least 30 minutes.

Once chilled, roll out the dough on a floured surface to fit a 9-inch pie dish. Transfer the dough to the pie dish and trim any excess dough from the edges. Crimp the edges as desired.

In a large mixing bowl, whisk together the pumpkin puree, coconut milk, brown sugar, cornstarch, vanilla extract, cinnamon, ginger, nutmeg, cloves, and salt until smooth and well combined.

Pour the filling into the prepared pie crust and smooth the top with a spatula.

Bake the pie in the preheated oven for 50-55 minutes, or until the filling is set and the crust is golden brown.

Remove the pie from the oven and let it cool completely on a wire rack before serving.

Serve slices of the egg-free pumpkin pie with whipped coconut cream or your favorite dairy-free topping. Enjoy!

Oatmeal Raisin Cookies

Ingredients:

- 1 cup rolled oats
- 3/4 cup all-purpose flour
- 1/2 teaspoon baking soda
- 1/2 teaspoon ground cinnamon
- 1/4 teaspoon salt
- 1/2 cup unsalted butter, softened
- 1/2 cup packed brown sugar
- 1/4 cup granulated sugar
- 1 large ripe banana, mashed
- 1 teaspoon vanilla extract
- 1/2 cup raisins

Instructions:

Preheat your oven to 350°F (175°C). Line a baking sheet with parchment paper or lightly grease it.

In a medium bowl, whisk together the rolled oats, flour, baking soda, cinnamon, and salt. Set aside.

In a large mixing bowl, cream together the softened butter, brown sugar, and granulated sugar until light and fluffy.

Add the mashed banana and vanilla extract to the butter-sugar mixture, and mix until well combined.

Gradually add the dry ingredients to the wet ingredients, stirring until just combined.

Fold in the raisins until evenly distributed throughout the dough.

Drop rounded tablespoons of dough onto the prepared baking sheet, leaving some space between each cookie.

Flatten each dough ball slightly with the back of a spoon or your fingers.

Bake in the preheated oven for 10 to 12 minutes, or until the cookies are golden brown around the edges.

Allow the cookies to cool on the baking sheet for a few minutes before transferring them to a wire rack to cool completely.

Enjoy your delicious egg-free oatmeal raisin cookies!

Lemon Drizzle Cake

Ingredients:

For the cake:

- 1 1/2 cups all-purpose flour
- 1 teaspoon baking powder
- 1/2 teaspoon baking soda
- 1/4 teaspoon salt
- 1/2 cup unsalted butter, softened
- 1 cup granulated sugar
- 2 large lemons, zest and juice
- 1/2 cup almond milk (or any other plant-based milk)
- 1 teaspoon vanilla extract

For the drizzle:

- 1/4 cup fresh lemon juice
- 1/4 cup granulated sugar

Instructions:

Preheat your oven to 350°F (175°C). Grease and line an 8-inch round cake pan with parchment paper.

In a medium bowl, whisk together the flour, baking powder, baking soda, and salt. Set aside.

In a large mixing bowl, cream together the softened butter and granulated sugar until light and fluffy.

Add the lemon zest and juice to the butter-sugar mixture, and mix until well combined.

Gradually add the dry ingredients to the wet ingredients, alternating with the almond milk, mixing until just combined. Stir in the vanilla extract.

Pour the batter into the prepared cake pan and spread it out evenly.

Bake in the preheated oven for 25 to 30 minutes, or until a toothpick inserted into the center comes out clean.

While the cake is baking, prepare the drizzle. In a small saucepan, heat the lemon juice and granulated sugar over medium heat until the sugar has dissolved, stirring occasionally. Remove from heat and set aside.

Once the cake is baked, remove it from the oven and let it cool in the pan for 10 minutes.

Use a skewer or toothpick to poke holes all over the top of the cake. Pour the lemon drizzle evenly over the warm cake, allowing it to soak in.
Allow the cake to cool completely in the pan before removing it and transferring it to a serving plate.
Slice and serve your delicious egg-free lemon drizzle cake!

Coconut Macaroons

Ingredients:

- 3 cups shredded coconut (sweetened or unsweetened, depending on preference)
- 3/4 cup sweetened condensed coconut milk
- 1 teaspoon vanilla extract
- 1/4 teaspoon salt
- 1/2 cup dairy-free chocolate chips (optional)

Instructions:

Preheat your oven to 350°F (175°C). Line a baking sheet with parchment paper.

In a large mixing bowl, combine the shredded coconut, sweetened condensed coconut milk, vanilla extract, and salt. Mix well until the ingredients are thoroughly combined.

If using chocolate chips, fold them into the coconut mixture.

Using a cookie scoop or tablespoon, scoop out portions of the coconut mixture and drop them onto the prepared baking sheet, spacing them a couple of inches apart.

Use your fingers or the back of a spoon to shape the coconut mixture into compact mounds.

Bake in the preheated oven for 10 to 12 minutes, or until the edges of the macaroons are golden brown.

Allow the macaroons to cool on the baking sheet for a few minutes before transferring them to a wire rack to cool completely.

If desired, melt some additional chocolate chips and drizzle it over the cooled macaroons for extra decoration.

Once the chocolate has set, your egg-free coconut macaroons are ready to enjoy! Store any leftovers in an airtight container at room temperature.

Raspberry Crumble Bars

Ingredients:

For the crust and crumble topping:

- 1 1/2 cups all-purpose flour
- 1/2 cup granulated sugar
- 1/4 teaspoon salt
- 3/4 cup unsalted butter, cold and cubed

For the raspberry filling:

- 2 cups fresh raspberries
- 1/4 cup granulated sugar
- 1 tablespoon cornstarch
- 1 tablespoon lemon juice

Instructions:

Preheat your oven to 350°F (175°C). Grease or line an 8x8 inch baking pan with parchment paper, leaving some overhang for easy removal.
In a large mixing bowl, combine the flour, sugar, and salt for the crust and crumble topping.
Add the cold, cubed butter to the flour mixture. Using a pastry cutter or your fingers, work the butter into the flour mixture until it resembles coarse crumbs. Some larger chunks of butter are okay.
Set aside about 1 cup of the crumb mixture to use as the topping later.
Press the remaining crumb mixture evenly into the bottom of the prepared baking pan to form the crust. Use the bottom of a glass or measuring cup to press it down firmly.
In a separate bowl, gently toss the raspberries with the granulated sugar, cornstarch, and lemon juice until the raspberries are coated.
Spread the raspberry mixture evenly over the crust in the baking pan.
Sprinkle the reserved crumb mixture evenly over the raspberry layer.
Bake in the preheated oven for 35 to 40 minutes, or until the top is golden brown and the raspberry filling is bubbly.
Remove the pan from the oven and let it cool completely on a wire rack.

Once cooled, use the parchment paper overhang to lift the bars out of the pan. Place them on a cutting board and slice into squares.
Serve and enjoy your delicious egg-free raspberry crumble bars! Store any leftovers in an airtight container at room temperature for up to several days.

Carrot Cake
Ingredients:
For the cake:

- 2 cups all-purpose flour
- 1 1/2 cups granulated sugar
- 1 teaspoon baking powder
- 1 teaspoon baking soda
- 1/2 teaspoon salt
- 1 teaspoon ground cinnamon
- 1/2 teaspoon ground nutmeg
- 1/2 teaspoon ground ginger
- 1 cup unsweetened applesauce
- 1/2 cup vegetable oil
- 1 teaspoon vanilla extract
- 2 cups grated carrots
- 1/2 cup crushed pineapple, drained

For the cream cheese frosting:

- 8 oz dairy-free cream cheese, softened
- 1/2 cup dairy-free butter, softened
- 3 cups powdered sugar
- 1 teaspoon vanilla extract

Instructions:

Preheat your oven to 350°F (175°C). Grease and flour two 9-inch round cake pans or line them with parchment paper.
In a large mixing bowl, whisk together the flour, sugar, baking powder, baking soda, salt, cinnamon, nutmeg, and ginger.
In another bowl, combine the applesauce, vegetable oil, and vanilla extract. Mix well.
Gradually add the wet ingredients to the dry ingredients, mixing until just combined.
Fold in the grated carrots and crushed pineapple until evenly distributed throughout the batter.
Divide the batter evenly between the prepared cake pans.
Bake in the preheated oven for 25 to 30 minutes, or until a toothpick inserted into the center comes out clean.
Allow the cakes to cool in the pans for 10 minutes, then transfer them to wire racks to cool completely.
While the cakes are cooling, prepare the cream cheese frosting. In a large mixing bowl, beat together the softened cream cheese and butter until smooth and creamy.

Gradually add the powdered sugar, beating until the frosting is smooth and spreadable. Mix in the vanilla extract.

Once the cakes are completely cooled, frost the top of one cake layer with a layer of cream cheese frosting. Place the second cake layer on top and frost the top and sides of the cake with the remaining frosting.

Slice and serve your delicious egg-free carrot cake! Store any leftovers in the refrigerator.

Peanut Butter Cookies

Ingredients:

- 1 cup creamy peanut butter
- 1 cup granulated sugar
- 1 teaspoon vanilla extract
- 1/4 cup unsweetened applesauce
- 1 1/4 cups all-purpose flour
- 1/2 teaspoon baking soda
- 1/4 teaspoon salt

Instructions:

Preheat your oven to 350°F (175°C). Line a baking sheet with parchment paper.
In a large mixing bowl, cream together the peanut butter, sugar, vanilla extract, and applesauce until smooth and well combined.
In a separate bowl, whisk together the flour, baking soda, and salt.
Gradually add the dry ingredients to the peanut butter mixture, mixing until a dough forms.
Roll the dough into tablespoon-sized balls and place them on the prepared baking sheet, spacing them about 2 inches apart.
Use a fork to flatten each dough ball, creating a criss-cross pattern on top.
Bake in the preheated oven for 10 to 12 minutes, or until the cookies are lightly golden brown around the edges.
Allow the cookies to cool on the baking sheet for a few minutes before transferring them to a wire rack to cool completely.
Enjoy your delicious egg-free peanut butter cookies!

Zucchini Bread

Ingredients:

- 2 cups shredded zucchini (about 1 medium zucchini)
- 1/2 cup unsweetened applesauce
- 1/2 cup vegetable oil
- 1 cup granulated sugar
- 1 teaspoon vanilla extract
- 2 cups all-purpose flour
- 1 teaspoon baking powder
- 1/2 teaspoon baking soda
- 1/2 teaspoon salt
- 1 teaspoon ground cinnamon
- 1/4 teaspoon ground nutmeg
- 1/2 cup chopped nuts (optional)

Instructions:

Preheat your oven to 350°F (175°C). Grease and flour a 9x5-inch loaf pan or line it with parchment paper.

In a large mixing bowl, combine the shredded zucchini, applesauce, vegetable oil, granulated sugar, and vanilla extract. Mix well.

In a separate bowl, whisk together the flour, baking powder, baking soda, salt, cinnamon, and nutmeg.

Gradually add the dry ingredients to the wet ingredients, stirring until just combined. Be careful not to overmix.

If using chopped nuts, fold them into the batter.

Pour the batter into the prepared loaf pan, spreading it out evenly.

Bake in the preheated oven for 50 to 60 minutes, or until a toothpick inserted into the center comes out clean.

Allow the zucchini bread to cool in the pan for 10 minutes, then transfer it to a wire rack to cool completely.

Slice and serve your delicious egg-free zucchini bread! Enjoy it warm or at room temperature.

Snickerdoodles

Ingredients:

- 2 3/4 cups all-purpose flour
- 2 teaspoons cream of tartar
- 1 teaspoon baking soda
- 1/4 teaspoon salt
- 1 cup unsalted butter, softened
- 1 1/2 cups granulated sugar
- 2 teaspoons vanilla extract
- 2 tablespoons unsweetened applesauce

For coating:

- 1/4 cup granulated sugar
- 2 teaspoons ground cinnamon

Instructions:

Preheat your oven to 375°F (190°C). Line baking sheets with parchment paper.
In a medium bowl, whisk together the flour, cream of tartar, baking soda, and salt. Set aside.
In a large mixing bowl, cream together the softened butter and sugar until light and fluffy.
Add the vanilla extract and unsweetened applesauce to the butter-sugar mixture, and mix until well combined.
Gradually add the dry ingredients to the wet ingredients, mixing until a dough forms.
In a small bowl, mix together the granulated sugar and ground cinnamon for the coating.
Use a cookie scoop or tablespoon to portion out dough and roll it into balls.
Roll each dough ball in the cinnamon-sugar mixture until coated.
Place the coated dough balls onto the prepared baking sheets, leaving some space between each cookie.
Gently flatten each dough ball with the bottom of a glass or the palm of your hand.
Bake in the preheated oven for 8 to 10 minutes, or until the edges are set and the tops are cracked.

Allow the cookies to cool on the baking sheets for a few minutes before transferring them to wire racks to cool completely.

Enjoy your delicious egg-free snickerdoodles! Store any leftovers in an airtight container at room temperature.

Apple Crisp

Ingredients:

For the filling:

- 6 cups peeled, cored, and sliced apples (about 6 medium-sized apples)
- 1/4 cup granulated sugar
- 2 tablespoons all-purpose flour
- 1 teaspoon ground cinnamon
- 1/4 teaspoon ground nutmeg
- 1 tablespoon lemon juice

For the crisp topping:

- 1 cup old-fashioned rolled oats
- 1/2 cup all-purpose flour
- 1/2 cup packed brown sugar
- 1/2 teaspoon ground cinnamon
- 1/4 teaspoon salt
- 1/2 cup unsalted butter, cold and cut into small pieces

Instructions:

Preheat your oven to 375°F (190°C). Grease a 9x13-inch baking dish or an equivalent-sized dish.

In a large mixing bowl, combine the sliced apples, granulated sugar, flour, cinnamon, nutmeg, and lemon juice. Toss until the apples are evenly coated, then transfer the mixture to the prepared baking dish.

In a separate bowl, combine the rolled oats, flour, brown sugar, cinnamon, and salt for the crisp topping. Mix well.

Add the cold butter pieces to the oat mixture. Use a pastry cutter or your fingers to work the butter into the dry ingredients until the mixture resembles coarse crumbs.

Sprinkle the crisp topping evenly over the apples in the baking dish.

Bake in the preheated oven for 40 to 45 minutes, or until the topping is golden brown and the apples are tender.

Allow the apple crisp to cool slightly before serving. Serve warm with a scoop of vanilla ice cream or a dollop of whipped cream, if desired.

Enjoy your delicious egg-free apple crisp!

Almond Butter Blondies

Ingredients:

- 1 cup almond butter
- 1/2 cup unsweetened applesauce
- 1/2 cup brown sugar
- 1/4 cup granulated sugar
- 2 teaspoons vanilla extract
- 1 cup all-purpose flour
- 1/2 teaspoon baking powder
- 1/4 teaspoon salt
- 1/2 cup dairy-free chocolate chips (optional)

Instructions:

Preheat your oven to 350°F (175°C). Grease or line an 8x8 inch baking pan with parchment paper.
In a large mixing bowl, combine the almond butter, applesauce, brown sugar, granulated sugar, and vanilla extract. Mix until smooth and well combined.
In a separate bowl, whisk together the flour, baking powder, and salt.
Gradually add the dry ingredients to the wet ingredients, mixing until just combined. Be careful not to overmix.
If using chocolate chips, fold them into the batter until evenly distributed.
Pour the batter into the prepared baking pan, spreading it out evenly.
Bake in the preheated oven for 20 to 25 minutes, or until the edges are golden brown and a toothpick inserted into the center comes out with a few moist crumbs.
Allow the blondies to cool in the pan for at least 15 minutes before slicing and serving.
Enjoy your delicious egg-free almond butter blondies!

Red Velvet Cupcakes

Ingredients:

For the cupcakes:

- 1 1/4 cups all-purpose flour
- 3/4 cup granulated sugar
- 1/2 teaspoon baking soda
- 1/2 teaspoon cocoa powder
- 1/2 teaspoon salt
- 1/2 cup vegetable oil
- 1/2 cup unsweetened almond milk (or any other plant-based milk)
- 1 tablespoon apple cider vinegar
- 1 teaspoon vanilla extract
- 1 tablespoon red food coloring

For the frosting:

- 8 oz dairy-free cream cheese, softened
- 1/2 cup dairy-free butter, softened
- 2 cups powdered sugar
- 1 teaspoon vanilla extract

Instructions:

Preheat your oven to 350°F (175°C). Line a muffin tin with cupcake liners.
In a large mixing bowl, whisk together the flour, sugar, baking soda, cocoa powder, and salt.
In a separate bowl, whisk together the vegetable oil, almond milk, apple cider vinegar, vanilla extract, and red food coloring.
Gradually add the wet ingredients to the dry ingredients, mixing until just combined.
Divide the batter evenly among the prepared cupcake liners, filling each about two-thirds full.
Bake in the preheated oven for 18 to 20 minutes, or until a toothpick inserted into the center of a cupcake comes out clean.
Remove the cupcakes from the oven and let them cool in the pan for a few minutes before transferring them to a wire rack to cool completely.
While the cupcakes are cooling, prepare the frosting. In a large mixing bowl, beat together the softened cream cheese and butter until smooth and creamy.

Gradually add the powdered sugar, beating until the frosting is smooth and spreadable. Mix in the vanilla extract.

Once the cupcakes are completely cooled, frost them with the cream cheese frosting.

Optionally, garnish with sprinkles or red velvet cake crumbs.

Serve and enjoy your delicious egg-free red velvet cupcakes!

Gingerbread Cookies

Ingredients:

- 3 cups all-purpose flour
- 1 teaspoon baking powder
- 1/2 teaspoon baking soda
- 1/4 teaspoon salt
- 1 tablespoon ground ginger
- 1 1/2 teaspoons ground cinnamon
- 1/2 teaspoon ground cloves
- 1/2 cup unsalted butter, softened
- 1/2 cup packed brown sugar
- 1/2 cup molasses
- 1 flax egg (1 tablespoon ground flaxseed meal + 3 tablespoons water)
- 1 teaspoon vanilla extract

Instructions:

In a medium bowl, whisk together the flour, baking powder, baking soda, salt, ginger, cinnamon, and cloves. Set aside.

In a large mixing bowl, cream together the softened butter and brown sugar until light and fluffy.

Add the molasses, flax egg, and vanilla extract to the butter-sugar mixture, and mix until well combined.

Gradually add the dry ingredients to the wet ingredients, mixing until a dough forms. If the dough is too sticky, you can add a little more flour.

Divide the dough in half, shape each half into a disk, wrap them in plastic wrap, and refrigerate for at least 1 hour (or overnight).

Preheat your oven to 350°F (175°C). Line baking sheets with parchment paper.

On a lightly floured surface, roll out one disk of dough to about 1/4 inch thickness. Use cookie cutters to cut out shapes.

Place the cut-out cookies onto the prepared baking sheets, leaving some space between each cookie.

Bake in the preheated oven for 8 to 10 minutes, or until the edges are set.

Allow the cookies to cool on the baking sheets for a few minutes before transferring them to wire racks to cool completely.

Once the cookies are cooled, you can decorate them with icing or enjoy them plain.

Repeat the process with the remaining dough.

Enjoy your delicious egg-free gingerbread cookies!

Strawberry Shortcake

Ingredients:

For the shortcakes:

- 2 cups all-purpose flour
- 1/4 cup granulated sugar
- 1 tablespoon baking powder
- 1/2 teaspoon salt
- 1/2 cup unsalted butter, cold and cubed
- 3/4 cup unsweetened almond milk (or any other plant-based milk)
- 1 teaspoon vanilla extract

For the strawberries:

- 4 cups fresh strawberries, hulled and sliced
- 2-3 tablespoons granulated sugar (adjust to taste)
- 1 tablespoon lemon juice

For the whipped cream:

- 1 can (13.5 oz) full-fat coconut cream, chilled in the refrigerator overnight
- 2-3 tablespoons powdered sugar (adjust to taste)
- 1 teaspoon vanilla extract

Instructions:

Preheat your oven to 425°F (220°C). Line a baking sheet with parchment paper.
In a large mixing bowl, whisk together the flour, sugar, baking powder, and salt.
Cut in the cold, cubed butter using a pastry cutter or your fingers until the mixture resembles coarse crumbs.
In a small bowl, mix together the almond milk and vanilla extract. Gradually add the milk mixture to the dry ingredients, stirring until just combined.
Turn the dough out onto a lightly floured surface and knead it gently a few times until it comes together.
Pat the dough into a rectangle about 3/4 inch thick. Use a biscuit cutter or a glass to cut out rounds of dough.
Place the dough rounds onto the prepared baking sheet. Gather any scraps of dough, pat them together, and cut out additional rounds.
Bake in the preheated oven for 12 to 15 minutes, or until the shortcakes are golden brown on top.

While the shortcakes are baking, prepare the strawberries. In a bowl, combine the sliced strawberries, granulated sugar (to taste), and lemon juice. Stir gently to coat the strawberries, then set aside to macerate.

Once the shortcakes are baked, remove them from the oven and let them cool on a wire rack.

While the shortcakes are cooling, prepare the whipped cream. Scoop the chilled coconut cream solids into a mixing bowl, leaving any liquid behind. Add the powdered sugar and vanilla extract, then beat with an electric mixer until fluffy.

To assemble, slice each shortcake in half horizontally. Place a spoonful of macerated strawberries on the bottom half of each shortcake, then top with a dollop of whipped cream. Place the top half of the shortcake on top.

Serve immediately and enjoy your delicious egg-free strawberry shortcake!

Pineapple Upside-Down Cake

Ingredients:

For the topping:

- 1/4 cup unsalted butter
- 3/4 cup packed brown sugar
- 1 can (20 oz) pineapple slices, drained
- Maraschino cherries (optional)

For the cake:

- 1 1/2 cups all-purpose flour
- 1 cup granulated sugar
- 1 teaspoon baking powder
- 1/2 teaspoon baking soda
- 1/4 teaspoon salt
- 1/2 cup unsweetened applesauce
- 1/4 cup vegetable oil
- 1 cup unsweetened pineapple juice
- 1 teaspoon vanilla extract

Instructions:

Preheat your oven to 350°F (175°C). Grease a 9-inch round cake pan.

In a small saucepan, melt the unsalted butter over medium heat. Add the brown sugar and stir until dissolved. Pour the mixture into the prepared cake pan.

Arrange the pineapple slices on top of the brown sugar mixture in the cake pan. You can also place a maraschino cherry in the center of each pineapple slice if desired.

In a large mixing bowl, whisk together the flour, granulated sugar, baking powder, baking soda, and salt.

In a separate bowl, combine the applesauce, vegetable oil, pineapple juice, and vanilla extract. Mix well.

Gradually add the wet ingredients to the dry ingredients, stirring until just combined.

Pour the batter over the pineapple slices in the cake pan, spreading it out evenly.

Bake in the preheated oven for 35 to 40 minutes, or until a toothpick inserted into the center comes out clean.

Remove the cake from the oven and let it cool in the pan for 5 minutes.

Place a serving plate upside down over the cake pan. Carefully flip the cake pan and plate together to invert the cake onto the serving plate. Be careful, as the pan and topping will be hot.

Allow the cake to cool slightly before slicing and serving.

Enjoy your delicious egg-free pineapple upside-down cake!

Cinnamon Rolls

Ingredients:

For the dough:

- 1 cup unsweetened almond milk (or any other plant-based milk)
- 1/4 cup vegetable oil
- 1/4 cup granulated sugar
- 1 packet (2 1/4 teaspoons) active dry yeast
- 3 cups all-purpose flour, plus more for dusting
- 1/2 teaspoon baking powder
- 1/2 teaspoon baking soda
- 1/2 teaspoon salt

For the filling:

- 1/2 cup packed brown sugar
- 2 tablespoons ground cinnamon
- 1/4 cup unsalted butter, softened

For the frosting:

- 4 oz dairy-free cream cheese, softened
- 1/4 cup dairy-free butter, softened
- 1 teaspoon vanilla extract
- 1 1/2 cups powdered sugar

Instructions:

In a small saucepan, heat the almond milk and vegetable oil over medium heat until just warm, about 110°F (43°C). Remove from heat and transfer to a mixing bowl.

Stir in the granulated sugar and sprinkle the yeast over the mixture. Let it sit for about 5 minutes until the yeast is foamy.

Add 2 1/2 cups of the flour to the yeast mixture, stirring until combined. Cover the bowl with a clean towel and let it rise in a warm place for about 1 hour, or until doubled in size.

Once the dough has risen, add the remaining 1/2 cup of flour, baking powder, baking soda, and salt. Stir until the dough comes together.

On a lightly floured surface, knead the dough for about 5 minutes until smooth and elastic.

Roll out the dough into a rectangle about 1/4 inch thick.

In a small bowl, mix together the brown sugar and cinnamon for the filling.

Spread the softened butter evenly over the rolled-out dough, then sprinkle the cinnamon-sugar mixture over the butter.

Starting from one long edge, tightly roll up the dough into a log. Pinch the seam to seal.

Cut the rolled dough into 12 equal-sized pieces.

Place the cinnamon rolls in a greased 9x13 inch baking dish, leaving some space between each roll.

Cover the baking dish with a clean towel and let the cinnamon rolls rise in a warm place for about 30 minutes.

Preheat your oven to 375°F (190°C). Bake the cinnamon rolls in the preheated oven for 20 to 25 minutes, or until golden brown.

While the cinnamon rolls are baking, prepare the frosting. In a mixing bowl, beat together the softened cream cheese, softened butter, and vanilla extract until smooth. Gradually add the powdered sugar and beat until creamy.

Once the cinnamon rolls are baked, remove them from the oven and let them cool slightly.

Spread the frosting over the warm cinnamon rolls and serve.

Enjoy your delicious egg-free cinnamon rolls!

Chocolate Cake

Ingredients:

- 1 1/2 cups all-purpose flour
- 1 cup granulated sugar
- 1/3 cup unsweetened cocoa powder
- 1 teaspoon baking soda
- 1/2 teaspoon salt
- 1 cup warm water
- 1/3 cup vegetable oil
- 1 tablespoon white vinegar
- 1 teaspoon vanilla extract

Instructions:

Preheat your oven to 350°F (175°C). Grease and flour a 9-inch round cake pan or line it with parchment paper.

In a large mixing bowl, sift together the flour, sugar, cocoa powder, baking soda, and salt.

In a separate bowl, whisk together the warm water, vegetable oil, vinegar, and vanilla extract.

Gradually add the wet ingredients to the dry ingredients, stirring until smooth and well combined.

Pour the batter into the prepared cake pan, spreading it out evenly.

Bake in the preheated oven for 25 to 30 minutes, or until a toothpick inserted into the center comes out clean.

Remove the cake from the oven and let it cool in the pan for 10 minutes before transferring it to a wire rack to cool completely.

Once the cake is cooled, you can frost it with your favorite frosting, dust it with powdered sugar, or serve it plain.

Enjoy your delicious egg-free chocolate cake!

Key Lime Pie

Ingredients:

For the crust:

- 1 1/2 cups graham cracker crumbs
- 1/4 cup granulated sugar
- 6 tablespoons unsalted butter, melted

For the filling:

- 4 large egg yolks
- 1 can (14 oz) sweetened condensed coconut milk
- 1/2 cup freshly squeezed key lime juice
- 1 tablespoon key lime zest

For the whipped cream topping:

- 1 cup chilled coconut cream (from a can of full-fat coconut milk)
- 2 tablespoons powdered sugar
- 1/2 teaspoon vanilla extract

Instructions:

Preheat your oven to 350°F (175°C). Grease a 9-inch pie dish.
In a medium bowl, combine the graham cracker crumbs, sugar, and melted butter. Mix until well combined.
Press the mixture firmly into the bottom and up the sides of the prepared pie dish to form the crust.
Bake the crust in the preheated oven for 10 minutes. Remove from the oven and let it cool while you prepare the filling.
In a large mixing bowl, whisk together the egg yolks and sweetened condensed coconut milk until smooth.
Add the key lime juice and zest to the egg mixture, and whisk until well combined.
Pour the filling into the cooled crust and spread it out evenly.
Bake the pie in the preheated oven for 15 to 20 minutes, or until the filling is set.
Remove the pie from the oven and let it cool completely on a wire rack. Once cooled, refrigerate the pie for at least 2 hours, or until chilled.
While the pie is chilling, prepare the whipped cream topping. In a mixing bowl, beat the chilled coconut cream, powdered sugar, and vanilla extract until stiff peaks form.

Once the pie is chilled, spread the whipped cream topping over the surface. Optionally, garnish the pie with additional lime zest or slices before serving. Slice and enjoy your delicious egg-free key lime pie!

Peanut Butter Banana Bread

Ingredients:

- 1 3/4 cups all-purpose flour
- 1 teaspoon baking powder
- 1/2 teaspoon baking soda
- 1/4 teaspoon salt
- 3 ripe bananas, mashed
- 1/2 cup creamy peanut butter
- 1/3 cup unsalted butter, melted
- 1/2 cup packed brown sugar
- 1/4 cup granulated sugar
- 2 large eggs
- 1 teaspoon vanilla extract

Instructions:

Preheat your oven to 350°F (175°C). Grease a 9x5-inch loaf pan.

In a large mixing bowl, whisk together the flour, baking powder, baking soda, and salt.

In another bowl, mix together the mashed bananas, peanut butter, melted butter, brown sugar, granulated sugar, eggs, and vanilla extract until well combined.

Gradually add the wet ingredients to the dry ingredients, stirring until just combined. Be careful not to overmix.

Pour the batter into the prepared loaf pan, spreading it out evenly.

Optional: If desired, you can sprinkle some additional granulated sugar or chopped peanuts on top of the batter for added texture.

Bake in the preheated oven for 50 to 60 minutes, or until a toothpick inserted into the center comes out clean.

If the bread starts to brown too quickly, you can loosely cover it with aluminum foil halfway through baking.

Once baked, remove the bread from the oven and let it cool in the pan for 10 minutes before transferring it to a wire rack to cool completely.

Slice and serve your delicious egg-free peanut butter banana bread! Enjoy it warm or at room temperature.

Black Forest Cake

Ingredients:

For the chocolate cake layers:

- 1 3/4 cups all-purpose flour
- 3/4 cup unsweetened cocoa powder
- 1 1/2 teaspoons baking powder
- 1 1/2 teaspoons baking soda
- 1 teaspoon salt
- 2 cups granulated sugar
- 2 large eggs
- 1 cup unsweetened almond milk (or any other plant-based milk)
- 1/2 cup vegetable oil
- 2 teaspoons vanilla extract
- 1 cup hot water

For the cherry filling:

- 3 cups pitted cherries (fresh or frozen)
- 1/2 cup granulated sugar
- 2 tablespoons cornstarch
- 1 tablespoon lemon juice

For the whipped cream frosting:

- 2 cups chilled coconut cream (from cans of full-fat coconut milk)
- 1/4 cup powdered sugar
- 1 teaspoon vanilla extract

For decoration:

- Dark chocolate shavings or curls
- Maraschino cherries

Instructions:

Preheat your oven to 350°F (175°C). Grease and flour two 9-inch round cake pans.
In a large mixing bowl, sift together the flour, cocoa powder, baking powder, baking soda, salt, and granulated sugar.

Add the eggs, almond milk, vegetable oil, and vanilla extract to the dry ingredients. Beat on medium speed until well combined.

Gradually add the hot water to the batter, mixing until smooth.

Divide the batter evenly between the prepared cake pans.

Bake in the preheated oven for 25 to 30 minutes, or until a toothpick inserted into the center comes out clean.

Allow the cakes to cool in the pans for 10 minutes, then transfer them to wire racks to cool completely.

While the cakes are cooling, prepare the cherry filling. In a saucepan, combine the pitted cherries, granulated sugar, cornstarch, and lemon juice. Cook over medium heat, stirring frequently, until the mixture thickens. Remove from heat and let it cool completely.

To make the whipped cream frosting, scoop the chilled coconut cream solids into a mixing bowl, leaving any liquid behind. Add the powdered sugar and vanilla extract. Beat with an electric mixer until stiff peaks form.

Once the cakes are cooled and the cherry filling and whipped cream frosting are ready, assemble the cake. Place one cake layer on a serving plate. Spread a layer of cherry filling over the cake layer. Top with a layer of whipped cream frosting. Place the second cake layer on top.

Frost the top and sides of the cake with the remaining whipped cream frosting.

Decorate the cake with dark chocolate shavings or curls and maraschino cherries.

Refrigerate the cake for at least 1 hour before serving to allow the flavors to meld.

Slice and serve your delicious egg-free black forest cake! Enjoy!

Lemon Poppy Seed Muffins

Ingredients:

- 2 cups all-purpose flour
- 3/4 cup granulated sugar
- 2 tablespoons poppy seeds
- 1 tablespoon baking powder
- 1/2 teaspoon baking soda
- 1/4 teaspoon salt
- 1 cup unsweetened almond milk (or any other plant-based milk)
- 1/2 cup vegetable oil
- 1/4 cup freshly squeezed lemon juice
- Zest of 1 lemon
- 2 teaspoons vanilla extract

For the glaze (optional):

- 1 cup powdered sugar
- 2-3 tablespoons freshly squeezed lemon juice

Instructions:

Preheat your oven to 375°F (190°C). Line a muffin tin with paper liners or grease it with non-stick cooking spray.

In a large mixing bowl, whisk together the flour, sugar, poppy seeds, baking powder, baking soda, and salt.

In a separate bowl, mix together the almond milk, vegetable oil, lemon juice, lemon zest, and vanilla extract.

Pour the wet ingredients into the dry ingredients and stir until just combined. Be careful not to overmix.

Spoon the batter into the prepared muffin tin, filling each muffin cup about two-thirds full.

Bake in the preheated oven for 18 to 20 minutes, or until a toothpick inserted into the center of a muffin comes out clean.

Remove the muffins from the oven and let them cool in the muffin tin for a few minutes before transferring them to a wire rack to cool completely.

If desired, prepare the glaze by whisking together the powdered sugar and lemon juice until smooth. Drizzle the glaze over the cooled muffins.

Allow the glaze to set before serving.

Enjoy your delicious egg-free lemon poppy seed muffins!

Sugar Cookies

Ingredients:

- 2 3/4 cups all-purpose flour
- 1 teaspoon baking soda
- 1/2 teaspoon baking powder
- 1 cup unsalted dairy-free butter, softened
- 1 1/2 cups granulated sugar
- 1 large flax egg (1 tablespoon ground flaxseed meal + 3 tablespoons water)
- 2 teaspoons vanilla extract
- 1/4 teaspoon almond extract (optional)
- 1/4 teaspoon salt

Instructions:

Preheat your oven to 375°F (190°C). Line baking sheets with parchment paper.

In a medium bowl, whisk together the flour, baking soda, and baking powder. Set aside.

In a large mixing bowl, cream together the softened dairy-free butter and granulated sugar until light and fluffy.

Add the flax egg, vanilla extract, almond extract (if using), and salt to the butter-sugar mixture. Beat until well combined.

Gradually add the dry ingredients to the wet ingredients, mixing until a dough forms.

Divide the dough into two equal portions. Flatten each portion into a disk, wrap them in plastic wrap, and chill in the refrigerator for at least 1 hour.

Once chilled, remove one disk of dough from the refrigerator. On a lightly floured surface, roll out the dough to about 1/4 inch thickness.

Use cookie cutters to cut out shapes from the dough. Place the cut-out cookies onto the prepared baking sheets, leaving some space between each cookie.

Gather any scraps of dough, re-roll, and cut out more cookies.

Bake in the preheated oven for 8 to 10 minutes, or until the edges are lightly golden brown.

Remove the cookies from the oven and let them cool on the baking sheets for a few minutes before transferring them to wire racks to cool completely.

Once cooled, you can decorate the cookies with icing or enjoy them plain.

Repeat the process with the remaining disk of dough.

Enjoy your delicious egg-free sugar cookies!

Coffee Cake

Ingredients:

For the cake:

- 2 cups all-purpose flour
- 1 cup granulated sugar
- 1/2 cup unsalted dairy-free butter, softened
- 1 cup unsweetened almond milk (or any other plant-based milk)
- 2 teaspoons baking powder
- 1 teaspoon vanilla extract
- 1/4 teaspoon salt

For the topping:

- 1/2 cup packed brown sugar
- 1/2 cup all-purpose flour
- 1/4 cup unsalted dairy-free butter, softened
- 1 tablespoon ground cinnamon

For the glaze:

- 1/2 cup powdered sugar
- 1-2 tablespoons unsweetened almond milk (or any other plant-based milk)
- 1/2 teaspoon vanilla extract

Instructions:

Preheat your oven to 350°F (175°C). Grease and flour a 9x9-inch baking pan.
In a large mixing bowl, cream together the softened dairy-free butter and granulated sugar until light and fluffy.
Add the almond milk and vanilla extract to the butter-sugar mixture, and mix until well combined.
In a separate bowl, whisk together the flour, baking powder, and salt.
Gradually add the dry ingredients to the wet ingredients, mixing until just combined.
Pour the batter into the prepared baking pan, spreading it out evenly.
In a small bowl, combine the brown sugar, flour, softened dairy-free butter, and ground cinnamon for the topping. Use a fork or your fingers to mix until crumbly.
Sprinkle the topping evenly over the cake batter in the baking pan.
Bake in the preheated oven for 30 to 35 minutes, or until a toothpick inserted into the center comes out clean.
While the cake is baking, prepare the glaze. In a small bowl, whisk together the powdered sugar, almond milk, and vanilla extract until smooth.

Once the cake is baked, remove it from the oven and let it cool in the pan for 10 minutes.
Drizzle the glaze over the warm cake.
Slice and serve your delicious egg-free coffee cake!

Almond Joy Bars

Ingredients:

For the crust:

- 1 1/2 cups graham cracker crumbs
- 1/2 cup unsalted dairy-free butter, melted

For the coconut filling:

- 2 cups shredded coconut
- 1 can (14 oz) sweetened condensed coconut milk

For the topping:

- 1 cup dairy-free chocolate chips
- 1/2 cup sliced almonds

Instructions:

Preheat your oven to 350°F (175°C). Line a 9x9-inch baking pan with parchment paper, leaving some overhang on the sides for easy removal.
In a medium bowl, mix together the graham cracker crumbs and melted dairy-free butter until well combined.
Press the mixture firmly into the bottom of the prepared baking pan to form the crust.
Bake the crust in the preheated oven for 8 to 10 minutes, or until lightly golden brown. Remove from the oven and let it cool slightly.
In a separate bowl, mix together the shredded coconut and sweetened condensed coconut milk until well combined.
Spread the coconut mixture evenly over the baked crust.
Return the pan to the oven and bake for an additional 20 to 25 minutes, or until the coconut is lightly golden brown.
Remove the pan from the oven and let it cool completely on a wire rack.
Once the bars are cooled, melt the dairy-free chocolate chips in the microwave or over a double boiler until smooth.
Pour the melted chocolate over the coconut layer and spread it out evenly with a spatula.
Sprinkle the sliced almonds over the melted chocolate.
Place the pan in the refrigerator for about 30 minutes, or until the chocolate is set.

Once the chocolate is set, use the parchment paper overhang to lift the bars out of the pan.

Slice the bars into squares or rectangles.

Serve and enjoy your delicious egg-free almond joy bars!

Raspberry Chocolate Tart

Ingredients:

For the crust:

- 1 1/2 cups all-purpose flour
- 1/2 cup powdered sugar
- 1/4 teaspoon salt
- 1/2 cup unsalted dairy-free butter, chilled and cubed
- 1 large flax egg (1 tablespoon ground flaxseed meal + 3 tablespoons water)
- 1 teaspoon vanilla extract

For the filling:

- 1 cup dairy-free chocolate chips
- 1/2 cup unsweetened almond milk (or any other plant-based milk)
- 1/2 teaspoon vanilla extract

For the topping:

- 2 cups fresh raspberries
- 2 tablespoons raspberry jam

Instructions:

Preheat your oven to 350°F (175°C). Grease a 9-inch tart pan with a removable bottom.
In a food processor, combine the flour, powdered sugar, and salt. Pulse until combined.
Add the chilled dairy-free butter to the food processor and pulse until the mixture resembles coarse crumbs.
In a small bowl, prepare the flax egg by mixing together the ground flaxseed meal and water. Let it sit for a few minutes to thicken.
Add the flax egg and vanilla extract to the food processor and pulse until the dough comes together.
Press the dough into the bottom and up the sides of the prepared tart pan, creating an even layer.
Prick the bottom of the crust with a fork to prevent it from puffing up during baking.
Bake the crust in the preheated oven for 20 to 25 minutes, or until lightly golden brown.
Remove the crust from the oven and let it cool completely on a wire rack.
While the crust is cooling, prepare the filling. In a small saucepan, heat the almond milk until it just begins to simmer.
Place the dairy-free chocolate chips in a heatproof bowl. Pour the hot almond milk over the chocolate chips and let it sit for 1 minute.
Add the vanilla extract to the chocolate mixture and stir until smooth and well combined.

Pour the chocolate filling into the cooled tart crust, spreading it out evenly.
Arrange the fresh raspberries on top of the chocolate filling.
In a small saucepan, heat the raspberry jam over low heat until melted. Brush the melted jam over the raspberries to glaze them.
Place the tart in the refrigerator for at least 1 hour, or until the chocolate filling is set.
Once set, remove the tart from the refrigerator and slice it into wedges.
Serve and enjoy your delicious egg-free raspberry chocolate tart!

Pistachio Baklava

Ingredients:

For the filling:

- 2 cups shelled pistachios, finely chopped
- 1/2 cup granulated sugar
- 1 teaspoon ground cinnamon
- 1/4 teaspoon ground cloves

For the syrup:

- 1 cup granulated sugar
- 1/2 cup water
- 1/4 cup honey
- 1 tablespoon lemon juice
- 1 cinnamon stick
- 1 teaspoon vanilla extract

For assembling:

- 1 package (16 oz) phyllo dough, thawed according to package instructions
- 1 cup unsalted dairy-free butter, melted

Instructions:

Preheat your oven to 350°F (175°C). Grease a 9x13-inch baking dish.

In a mixing bowl, combine the finely chopped pistachios, granulated sugar, ground cinnamon, and ground cloves. Mix well and set aside.

In a saucepan, combine the granulated sugar, water, honey, lemon juice, cinnamon stick, and vanilla extract for the syrup. Bring the mixture to a boil over medium heat, stirring occasionally. Once boiling, reduce the heat and let it simmer for about 5 minutes. Remove from heat and set aside to cool.

Unroll the thawed phyllo dough and place it between two damp kitchen towels to prevent it from drying out.

Place one sheet of phyllo dough in the prepared baking dish and brush it lightly with melted dairy-free butter. Repeat with several more sheets of phyllo dough, brushing each layer with melted butter.

Sprinkle a generous layer of the pistachio filling evenly over the buttered phyllo dough.

Continue layering phyllo dough and butter until all the dough and filling are used, finishing with a top layer of phyllo dough. Make sure to brush the top layer generously with melted butter.

Using a sharp knife, carefully cut the baklava into diamond or square-shaped pieces.

Bake in the preheated oven for 45 to 50 minutes, or until the baklava is golden brown and crisp.

Remove the baklava from the oven and immediately pour the cooled syrup over the hot baklava, making sure to cover all the pieces.

Allow the baklava to cool completely in the baking dish before serving.

Serve and enjoy your delicious egg-free pistachio baklava!

Churros

Ingredients:

For the churros:

- 1 cup water
- 2 tablespoons granulated sugar
- 1/2 teaspoon salt
- 2 tablespoons vegetable oil
- 1 cup all-purpose flour
- Vegetable oil, for frying

For the cinnamon sugar coating:

- 1/2 cup granulated sugar
- 1 teaspoon ground cinnamon

For the chocolate dipping sauce (optional):

- 1/2 cup dairy-free chocolate chips
- 1/4 cup unsweetened almond milk (or any other plant-based milk)
- 1/2 teaspoon vanilla extract

Instructions:

In a saucepan, combine the water, sugar, salt, and vegetable oil. Bring the mixture to a boil over medium heat.
Once boiling, remove the saucepan from the heat and add the flour all at once. Stir vigorously until the mixture forms a ball of dough.
Transfer the dough to a piping bag fitted with a star tip.
In a shallow bowl, mix together the granulated sugar and ground cinnamon for the coating.
In a separate saucepan, heat vegetable oil for frying over medium-high heat until it reaches 375°F (190°C).
Pipe 4 to 6-inch strips of dough directly into the hot oil, using scissors to cut the dough from the piping bag. Be careful not to overcrowd the pan.
Fry the churros for 2 to 3 minutes on each side, or until golden brown and crisp. Use a slotted spoon to remove them from the oil and transfer them to a plate lined with paper towels to drain excess oil.
While the churros are still warm, roll them in the cinnamon sugar mixture to coat evenly.

Repeat the frying and coating process with the remaining dough.
If making chocolate dipping sauce, combine the dairy-free chocolate chips and almond milk in a microwave-safe bowl. Microwave in 30-second intervals, stirring in between, until the chocolate is melted and smooth. Stir in the vanilla extract.
Serve the warm churros with the chocolate dipping sauce on the side, if desired.
Enjoy your delicious egg-free churros!

Marble Pound Cake

Ingredients:

- 1 3/4 cups all-purpose flour
- 1 teaspoon baking powder
- 1/2 teaspoon salt
- 1/2 cup unsalted dairy-free butter, softened
- 1 cup granulated sugar
- 3 large flax eggs (3 tablespoons ground flaxseed meal + 9 tablespoons water)
- 1 teaspoon vanilla extract
- 1/3 cup unsweetened cocoa powder
- 1/4 cup unsweetened almond milk (or any other plant-based milk)

Instructions:

Preheat your oven to 350°F (175°C). Grease and flour a 9x5-inch loaf pan.
In a medium bowl, sift together the flour, baking powder, and salt. Set aside.
In a large mixing bowl, cream together the softened dairy-free butter and granulated sugar until light and fluffy.
Add the flax eggs, one at a time, beating well after each addition. Stir in the vanilla extract.
Gradually add the dry ingredients to the wet ingredients, mixing until just combined.
In a separate bowl, mix the unsweetened cocoa powder and almond milk until smooth.
Remove 1 cup of the batter and mix it with the cocoa mixture to create the chocolate batter.
Alternately spoon dollops of the vanilla and chocolate batters into the prepared loaf pan.
Once all the batter is in the pan, use a knife or skewer to gently swirl the batters together to create a marbled effect.
Bake in the preheated oven for 50 to 60 minutes, or until a toothpick inserted into the center comes out clean.
Remove the pound cake from the oven and let it cool in the pan for 10 minutes before transferring it to a wire rack to cool completely.
Once cooled, slice and serve your delicious egg-free marble pound cake!

Oreo Cheesecake

Ingredients:

For the crust:

- 24 Oreo cookies
- 1/4 cup unsalted dairy-free butter, melted

For the cheesecake filling:

- 24 oz dairy-free cream cheese, softened
- 1 cup granulated sugar
- 1/4 cup unsweetened almond milk (or any other plant-based milk)
- 2 teaspoons vanilla extract
- 3 tablespoons cornstarch
- 1/2 cup dairy-free sour cream

For the Oreo topping:

- 12 Oreo cookies, crushed

Instructions:

Preheat your oven to 325°F (160°C). Grease a 9-inch springform pan.
Crush the Oreo cookies for the crust in a food processor until fine crumbs form.
In a mixing bowl, combine the Oreo crumbs with the melted dairy-free butter. Press the mixture evenly into the bottom of the prepared springform pan.
In a large mixing bowl, beat the softened dairy-free cream cheese and granulated sugar until smooth and creamy.
Add the almond milk, vanilla extract, and cornstarch to the cream cheese mixture. Beat until well combined and smooth.
Fold in the dairy-free sour cream until fully incorporated.
Pour the cheesecake filling over the prepared Oreo crust in the springform pan, spreading it out evenly.
Tap the pan on the counter a few times to release any air bubbles.
Sprinkle the crushed Oreo cookies over the top of the cheesecake filling.
Place the springform pan on a baking sheet and bake in the preheated oven for 45 to 50 minutes, or until the edges are set and the center is slightly jiggly.
Turn off the oven and leave the cheesecake inside with the oven door closed for 1 hour.
Remove the cheesecake from the oven and let it cool completely on a wire rack.
Once cooled, refrigerate the cheesecake for at least 4 hours or overnight to set.
Before serving, run a knife around the edge of the springform pan to loosen the cheesecake, then release the sides of the pan.

Slice and serve your delicious egg-free Oreo cheesecake!

Salted Caramel Brownies

Ingredients:

For the brownie base:

- 1 cup all-purpose flour
- 3/4 cup cocoa powder
- 1/2 teaspoon baking powder
- 1/2 teaspoon salt
- 3/4 cup unsalted dairy-free butter, melted
- 1 1/2 cups granulated sugar
- 3 large flax eggs (3 tablespoons ground flaxseed meal + 9 tablespoons water)
- 1 teaspoon vanilla extract

For the salted caramel sauce:

- 1 cup granulated sugar
- 6 tablespoons unsalted dairy-free butter
- 1/2 cup full-fat coconut milk
- 1/2 teaspoon sea salt

Instructions:

Preheat your oven to 350°F (175°C). Grease and line a 9x9-inch baking pan with parchment paper, leaving some overhang on the sides for easy removal.
In a medium bowl, whisk together the flour, cocoa powder, baking powder, and salt. Set aside.
In a large mixing bowl, whisk together the melted dairy-free butter, granulated sugar, flax eggs, and vanilla extract until smooth and well combined.
Gradually add the dry ingredients to the wet ingredients, mixing until just combined.
Pour the brownie batter into the prepared baking pan, spreading it out evenly.
In a medium saucepan, heat the granulated sugar over medium heat, stirring constantly with a rubber spatula or wooden spoon. The sugar will clump up and eventually melt into a thick, amber-colored liquid as you continue to stir.
Once the sugar is fully melted and golden brown, add the dairy-free butter to the saucepan and stir until melted and combined.
Slowly pour in the coconut milk while stirring constantly. Be careful as the mixture will bubble up.

Allow the mixture to boil for 1 minute, then remove it from the heat and stir in the sea salt.

Pour the salted caramel sauce evenly over the brownie batter in the baking pan.

Use a knife or skewer to swirl the salted caramel into the brownie batter to create a marbled effect.

Bake in the preheated oven for 25 to 30 minutes, or until the edges are set and a toothpick inserted into the center comes out with a few moist crumbs.

Remove the brownies from the oven and let them cool completely in the pan on a wire rack.

Once cooled, lift the brownies out of the pan using the parchment paper overhang and transfer them to a cutting board.

Slice the brownies into squares and serve.

Enjoy your delicious egg-free salted caramel brownies!

Cherry Pie
Ingredients:
For the crust:

- 2 1/2 cups all-purpose flour
- 1 teaspoon salt
- 1 tablespoon granulated sugar
- 1 cup unsalted dairy-free butter, chilled and cubed
- 6-8 tablespoons ice water

For the cherry filling:

- 6 cups fresh or frozen cherries, pitted
- 3/4 cup granulated sugar
- 1/4 cup cornstarch
- 1 tablespoon lemon juice
- 1/2 teaspoon almond extract
- 1/4 teaspoon salt
- 1 tablespoon unsalted dairy-free butter, cubed

Instructions:

To make the crust, in a food processor, combine the flour, salt, and granulated sugar. Pulse a few times to mix.
Add the chilled dairy-free butter cubes to the food processor and pulse until the mixture resembles coarse crumbs.
Gradually add the ice water, 1 tablespoon at a time, pulsing until the dough just comes together. Be careful not to overmix.
Divide the dough into two equal portions, flatten each into a disk, wrap in plastic wrap, and refrigerate for at least 1 hour.
Preheat your oven to 400°F (200°C). Grease a 9-inch pie dish.
In a large mixing bowl, combine the pitted cherries, granulated sugar, cornstarch, lemon juice, almond extract, and salt. Stir until the cherries are coated evenly.
Roll out one disk of the chilled dough on a lightly floured surface to fit the bottom of the pie dish. Place it in the prepared dish.
Pour the cherry filling into the pie crust, spreading it out evenly.
Dot the top of the filling with cubed dairy-free butter.
Roll out the second disk of dough and place it over the cherry filling. You can either leave it whole or cut it into strips for a lattice crust.

If using a whole top crust, make several slits in the center to allow steam to escape.
If making a lattice crust, weave the strips over the filling.
Trim any excess dough from the edges and crimp the edges to seal.
Optionally, brush the top crust with a little almond milk and sprinkle with granulated sugar for a golden finish.
Place the pie on a baking sheet to catch any drips and bake in the preheated oven for 45 to 50 minutes, or until the crust is golden brown and the filling is bubbling.
If the edges of the crust start to brown too quickly, you can cover them with aluminum foil halfway through baking.
Once baked, remove the pie from the oven and let it cool on a wire rack before slicing and serving.
Serve your delicious egg-free cherry pie warm or at room temperature. Enjoy!

Almond Biscotti

Ingredients:

- 2 cups all-purpose flour
- 1 cup granulated sugar
- 1 teaspoon baking powder
- 1/4 teaspoon salt
- 1/2 cup unsalted dairy-free butter, melted
- 2 flax eggs (2 tablespoons ground flaxseed meal + 6 tablespoons water)
- 1 teaspoon almond extract
- 1 cup whole almonds, toasted

Instructions:

Preheat your oven to 350°F (175°C). Line a baking sheet with parchment paper.
In a large mixing bowl, whisk together the flour, sugar, baking powder, and salt.
In a separate bowl, prepare the flax eggs by mixing together the ground flaxseed meal and water. Let it sit for a few minutes to thicken.
Add the melted dairy-free butter, flax eggs, and almond extract to the dry ingredients. Stir until well combined.
Fold in the toasted whole almonds until evenly distributed throughout the dough.
Divide the dough in half. Shape each half into a log about 12 inches long and 2 inches wide. Place the logs on the prepared baking sheet, leaving space between them.
Bake in the preheated oven for 25 to 30 minutes, or until the logs are firm to the touch and lightly golden brown.
Remove the baking sheet from the oven and let the logs cool for 10 minutes.
Reduce the oven temperature to 325°F (160°C).
Using a serrated knife, carefully slice the logs diagonally into 1/2-inch thick slices.
Arrange the biscotti slices cut-side down on the baking sheet.
Bake for an additional 10 to 15 minutes, or until the biscotti are crisp and golden brown.
Remove the baking sheet from the oven and let the biscotti cool completely on a wire rack.
Once cooled, store the almond biscotti in an airtight container at room temperature.
Enjoy your delicious egg-free almond biscotti with a cup of coffee or tea!

Fig Newtons
Ingredients:
For the dough:

- 1 1/2 cups all-purpose flour
- 1/2 cup whole wheat flour
- 1/2 teaspoon baking powder
- 1/4 teaspoon salt
- 1/2 cup unsalted dairy-free butter, softened
- 1/2 cup granulated sugar
- 1 flax egg (1 tablespoon ground flaxseed meal + 3 tablespoons water)
- 1 teaspoon vanilla extract

For the fig filling:

- 1 1/2 cups dried figs, stems removed and chopped
- 1/2 cup water
- 2 tablespoons granulated sugar
- 1 tablespoon lemon juice
- 1/2 teaspoon lemon zest

Instructions:

Preheat your oven to 350°F (175°C). Line a baking sheet with parchment paper.
In a medium saucepan, combine the chopped dried figs, water, granulated sugar, lemon juice, and lemon zest. Bring the mixture to a simmer over medium heat. Reduce the heat to low and let the mixture simmer for 5 to 7 minutes, or until the figs are soft and the mixture has thickened slightly.
Remove the saucepan from the heat and let the fig filling cool slightly. Once cooled, transfer the filling to a food processor or blender and pulse until smooth. Set aside.
In a large mixing bowl, cream together the softened dairy-free butter and granulated sugar until light and fluffy.
Add the flax egg and vanilla extract to the butter-sugar mixture and beat until well combined.
In a separate bowl, whisk together the all-purpose flour, whole wheat flour, baking powder, and salt.
Gradually add the dry ingredients to the wet ingredients, mixing until a dough forms.

Divide the dough into two equal portions. Roll out one portion of the dough between two sheets of parchment paper to form a rectangle about 1/4 inch thick.
Spread half of the fig filling evenly over the rolled-out dough.
Carefully roll up the dough into a log, using the parchment paper to help guide you. Repeat with the remaining dough and fig filling.
Place the rolled dough logs seam-side down on the prepared baking sheet.
Bake in the preheated oven for 20 to 25 minutes, or until the dough is golden brown.
Remove the baking sheet from the oven and let the fig rolls cool for 10 minutes.
Use a sharp knife to slice the rolls into individual Fig Newtons, about 1 inch thick.
Place the sliced Fig Newtons back on the baking sheet and return them to the oven for an additional 5 to 10 minutes, or until they are firm to the touch.
Remove the Fig Newtons from the oven and let them cool completely on a wire rack before serving.
Enjoy your delicious egg-free Fig Newtons as a snack or dessert!

Scones

Ingredients:

- 2 cups all-purpose flour
- 1/4 cup granulated sugar
- 1 tablespoon baking powder
- 1/2 teaspoon salt
- 1/2 cup unsalted dairy-free butter, cold and cubed
- 1/2 cup unsweetened almond milk (or any other plant-based milk)
- 1 teaspoon vanilla extract
- 1 flax egg (1 tablespoon ground flaxseed meal + 3 tablespoons water)
- Optional: 1/2 cup add-ins such as dried fruit, chocolate chips, or nuts

Instructions:

Preheat your oven to 400°F (200°C). Line a baking sheet with parchment paper.
In a large mixing bowl, whisk together the flour, sugar, baking powder, and salt.
Add the cold, cubed dairy-free butter to the dry ingredients. Using a pastry cutter or your fingers, cut the butter into the flour mixture until it resembles coarse crumbs.
In a separate bowl, whisk together the almond milk, vanilla extract, and flax egg.
Pour the wet ingredients into the dry ingredients and mix until just combined. If adding any optional add-ins, gently fold them into the dough.
Turn the dough out onto a lightly floured surface and knead it a few times until it comes together. Be careful not to overwork the dough.
Pat the dough into a circle about 1 inch thick.
Use a sharp knife or a biscuit cutter to cut the dough into wedges or rounds, depending on your preference.
Place the scones on the prepared baking sheet, leaving some space between each one.
Optional: Brush the tops of the scones with a little almond milk or melted dairy-free butter for a golden finish.
Bake in the preheated oven for 12 to 15 minutes, or until the scones are lightly golden brown.
Remove the scones from the oven and let them cool on the baking sheet for a few minutes before transferring them to a wire rack to cool completely.
Serve the scones warm or at room temperature with your favorite toppings such as jam, vegan butter, or dairy-free cream.
Enjoy your delicious egg-free scones for breakfast or as a snack!

Coconut Cream Pie

Ingredients:

For the crust:

- 1 1/2 cups graham cracker crumbs
- 1/3 cup granulated sugar
- 1/2 cup unsalted dairy-free butter, melted

For the coconut cream filling:

- 1 can (13.5 oz) full-fat coconut milk
- 1 cup unsweetened coconut milk beverage (from a carton)
- 1/2 cup granulated sugar
- 1/4 cup cornstarch
- 1/4 teaspoon salt
- 1 teaspoon vanilla extract
- 1 cup shredded coconut

For the topping:

- 1 1/2 cups coconut whipped cream (store-bought or homemade)
- Toasted coconut flakes, for garnish (optional)

Instructions:

Preheat your oven to 350°F (175°C). Grease a 9-inch pie dish.

In a mixing bowl, combine the graham cracker crumbs, granulated sugar, and melted dairy-free butter. Mix until well combined.

Press the mixture into the bottom and up the sides of the prepared pie dish to form the crust.

Bake the crust in the preheated oven for 10 minutes. Remove from the oven and let it cool completely on a wire rack.

In a medium saucepan, combine the full-fat coconut milk, coconut milk beverage, granulated sugar, cornstarch, and salt for the filling. Whisk until smooth.

Place the saucepan over medium heat and cook, stirring constantly, until the mixture thickens and comes to a simmer.

Once the mixture has thickened, remove it from the heat and stir in the vanilla extract and shredded coconut.

Pour the coconut cream filling into the cooled pie crust, spreading it out evenly.

Place the pie in the refrigerator and chill for at least 4 hours, or until the filling is set.
Once the filling is set, spread the coconut whipped cream over the top of the pie.
Garnish with toasted coconut flakes, if desired.
Slice and serve your delicious egg-free coconut cream pie chilled.
Enjoy!

Vanilla Cupcakes
Ingredients:

- 1 1/2 cups all-purpose flour
- 1 1/2 teaspoons baking powder
- 1/4 teaspoon salt
- 1/2 cup unsalted dairy-free butter, softened
- 1 cup granulated sugar
- 2 flax eggs (2 tablespoons ground flaxseed meal + 6 tablespoons water)
- 2 teaspoons vanilla extract
- 1/2 cup unsweetened almond milk (or any other plant-based milk)

Instructions:

Preheat your oven to 350°F (175°C). Line a muffin tin with cupcake liners.
In a medium bowl, whisk together the flour, baking powder, and salt. Set aside.
In a large mixing bowl, cream together the softened dairy-free butter and granulated sugar until light and fluffy.
Add the flax eggs and vanilla extract to the butter-sugar mixture. Beat until well combined.
Gradually add the dry ingredients to the wet ingredients, alternating with the almond milk, mixing until just combined. Be careful not to overmix.
Fill each cupcake liner about 2/3 full with the batter.
Bake in the preheated oven for 18 to 20 minutes, or until a toothpick inserted into the center of a cupcake comes out clean.
Remove the cupcakes from the oven and let them cool in the muffin tin for a few minutes before transferring them to a wire rack to cool completely.
Once cooled, decorate the cupcakes with your favorite frosting or toppings, if desired.
Serve and enjoy your delicious egg-free vanilla cupcakes!

Chocolate Babka

Ingredients:

For the dough:

- 3 1/2 cups all-purpose flour
- 1/2 cup granulated sugar
- 2 1/4 teaspoons active dry yeast
- 1 teaspoon salt
- 3/4 cup unsweetened almond milk (or any other plant-based milk), warmed to about 110°F (45°C)
- 1/2 cup unsalted dairy-free butter, melted
- 2 flax eggs (2 tablespoons ground flaxseed meal + 6 tablespoons water)
- 1 teaspoon vanilla extract

For the chocolate filling:

- 1/2 cup granulated sugar
- 1/2 cup unsweetened cocoa powder
- 1/4 cup unsalted dairy-free butter, melted
- 1 teaspoon vanilla extract

For the streusel topping (optional):

- 1/4 cup all-purpose flour
- 1/4 cup granulated sugar
- 2 tablespoons unsalted dairy-free butter, cold

For the syrup:

- 1/4 cup water
- 1/4 cup granulated sugar

Instructions:

In a large mixing bowl, combine the flour, sugar, yeast, and salt.
In a separate bowl, whisk together the warmed almond milk, melted dairy-free butter, flax eggs, and vanilla extract.
Pour the wet ingredients into the dry ingredients and mix until a dough forms. Knead the dough on a lightly floured surface for about 5 minutes, until smooth and elastic.

Place the dough in a greased bowl, cover with a clean kitchen towel, and let it rise in a warm place for about 1 hour, or until doubled in size.

In the meantime, prepare the chocolate filling by mixing together the granulated sugar, cocoa powder, melted dairy-free butter, and vanilla extract in a bowl until well combined. Set aside.

If making the streusel topping, combine the flour and sugar in a bowl. Cut in the cold dairy-free butter using a pastry cutter or fork until the mixture resembles coarse crumbs. Set aside.

Once the dough has doubled in size, punch it down and divide it in half.

Roll out one half of the dough on a lightly floured surface into a rectangle about 1/4 inch thick.

Spread half of the chocolate filling evenly over the rolled-out dough.

Roll up the dough tightly from one of the long sides to form a log.

Repeat the rolling, filling, and rolling process with the other half of the dough and remaining chocolate filling.

If using the streusel topping, sprinkle it over the top of each babka loaf.

Place each rolled babka dough into a greased loaf pan, cover with a clean kitchen towel, and let them rise in a warm place for another 30 minutes.

Preheat your oven to 350°F (175°C).

Bake the babka loaves in the preheated oven for 30 to 35 minutes, or until golden brown and cooked through.

While the babka is baking, prepare the syrup by combining the water and sugar in a small saucepan. Bring to a boil, then remove from heat and set aside to cool slightly.

Once the babka loaves are baked, remove them from the oven and immediately brush the syrup over the top of each loaf.

Let the babka cool in the loaf pans for about 10 minutes before transferring them to a wire rack to cool completely.

Slice and serve your delicious egg-free chocolate babka. Enjoy!

Pumpkin Roll

Ingredients:

For the pumpkin cake:

- 3/4 cup all-purpose flour
- 1/2 teaspoon baking powder
- 1/2 teaspoon baking soda
- 1/2 teaspoon ground cinnamon
- 1/4 teaspoon ground nutmeg
- 1/4 teaspoon ground cloves
- 1/4 teaspoon salt
- 3 large eggs
- 1 cup granulated sugar
- 2/3 cup canned pumpkin puree

For the filling:

- 1 cup powdered sugar, sifted
- 8 oz dairy-free cream cheese, softened
- 1/4 cup dairy-free butter, softened
- 1 teaspoon vanilla extract

For dusting:

- Powdered sugar, for dusting

Instructions:

Preheat your oven to 375°F (190°C). Grease a 10x15-inch jelly roll pan and line it with parchment paper, leaving some overhang on the sides.
In a medium bowl, sift together the flour, baking powder, baking soda, cinnamon, nutmeg, cloves, and salt. Set aside.
In a large mixing bowl, beat the eggs and granulated sugar together until pale and fluffy.
Add the pumpkin puree to the egg mixture and mix until well combined.
Gradually add the dry ingredients to the wet ingredients, mixing until just combined.
Spread the batter evenly into the prepared jelly roll pan.
Bake in the preheated oven for 12 to 15 minutes, or until the cake is set and springs back when lightly touched.

While the cake is baking, lay a clean kitchen towel flat on the counter and sprinkle it generously with powdered sugar.

Once the cake is done baking, immediately invert it onto the prepared kitchen towel.

Carefully peel off the parchment paper and discard.

Starting at the short end, carefully roll up the cake with the towel, rolling it tightly but gently. Let it cool completely on a wire rack, seam-side down.

While the cake is cooling, prepare the filling by beating together the powdered sugar, dairy-free cream cheese, dairy-free butter, and vanilla extract until smooth and creamy.

Once the cake is completely cooled, carefully unroll it from the towel.

Spread the cream cheese filling evenly over the surface of the cake, leaving a small border around the edges.

Carefully re-roll the cake, this time without the towel. Use the towel to help you if needed.

Wrap the pumpkin roll in plastic wrap and refrigerate for at least 1 hour before serving.

Before serving, dust the pumpkin roll with powdered sugar.

Slice and serve your delicious egg-free pumpkin roll. Enjoy!

Mocha Cake
Ingredients:
For the cake:

- 1 3/4 cups all-purpose flour
- 3/4 cup unsweetened cocoa powder
- 1 1/2 teaspoons baking powder
- 1 1/2 teaspoons baking soda
- 1/2 teaspoon salt
- 1 3/4 cups granulated sugar
- 2 flax eggs (2 tablespoons ground flaxseed meal + 6 tablespoons water)
- 1 cup unsweetened almond milk (or any other plant-based milk)
- 1/2 cup vegetable oil
- 2 teaspoons vanilla extract
- 1 cup hot brewed coffee (or espresso), cooled

For the frosting:

- 1/2 cup dairy-free butter, softened
- 2 cups powdered sugar, sifted
- 1/4 cup unsweetened cocoa powder
- 1-2 tablespoons unsweetened almond milk (or any other plant-based milk)
- 1 teaspoon instant coffee granules
- 1 teaspoon vanilla extract

For garnish (optional):

- Chocolate shavings
- Espresso beans

Instructions:

Preheat your oven to 350°F (175°C). Grease and flour two 9-inch round cake pans.
In a large mixing bowl, sift together the flour, cocoa powder, baking powder, baking soda, salt, and granulated sugar.
In another mixing bowl, prepare the flax eggs by mixing together the ground flaxseed meal and water. Let it sit for a few minutes to thicken.
Add the flax eggs, almond milk, vegetable oil, and vanilla extract to the dry ingredients. Beat on medium speed until well combined.

Gradually add the hot brewed coffee to the batter, mixing until smooth. The batter will be thin.

Divide the batter evenly between the prepared cake pans.

Bake in the preheated oven for 25 to 30 minutes, or until a toothpick inserted into the center of the cakes comes out clean.

Remove the cakes from the oven and let them cool in the pans for 10 minutes before transferring them to wire racks to cool completely.

While the cakes are cooling, prepare the frosting. In a mixing bowl, beat the softened dairy-free butter until creamy.

Gradually add the powdered sugar and cocoa powder, mixing until well combined.

Dissolve the instant coffee granules in 1 tablespoon of almond milk, then add it to the frosting mixture along with the vanilla extract. Beat until smooth and creamy, adding more almond milk if needed to reach your desired consistency.

Once the cakes are completely cooled, place one layer on a serving plate or cake stand. Spread a layer of frosting evenly over the top.

Place the second cake layer on top and frost the top and sides of the cake with the remaining frosting.

Garnish the cake with chocolate shavings and espresso beans, if desired.

Slice and serve your delicious egg-free mocha cake. Enjoy!

Lemon Bars

Ingredients:

For the crust:

- 1 cup all-purpose flour
- 1/4 cup powdered sugar
- 1/2 cup unsalted dairy-free butter, softened

For the lemon filling:

- 1 cup granulated sugar
- 2 tablespoons all-purpose flour
- 1/2 teaspoon baking powder
- Pinch of salt
- 2 flax eggs (2 tablespoons ground flaxseed meal + 6 tablespoons water)
- 1/3 cup fresh lemon juice
- Zest of 1 lemon

For dusting (optional):

- Powdered sugar, for dusting

Instructions:

Preheat your oven to 350°F (175°C). Grease an 8x8-inch baking pan and line it with parchment paper, leaving some overhang on the sides for easy removal.
In a mixing bowl, combine the flour, powdered sugar, and softened dairy-free butter for the crust. Mix until the mixture resembles coarse crumbs.
Press the crust mixture evenly into the bottom of the prepared baking pan.
Bake the crust in the preheated oven for 15 to 20 minutes, or until lightly golden brown.
While the crust is baking, prepare the lemon filling. In a medium bowl, whisk together the granulated sugar, flour, baking powder, and salt.
Add the flax eggs, fresh lemon juice, and lemon zest to the dry ingredients. Whisk until well combined and smooth.
Once the crust is baked, remove it from the oven and pour the lemon filling over the hot crust.
Return the pan to the oven and bake for an additional 20 to 25 minutes, or until the filling is set and the edges are lightly golden brown.

Remove the lemon bars from the oven and let them cool completely in the pan on a wire rack.
Once cooled, refrigerate the lemon bars for at least 1 hour to chill and set.
Once chilled, use the parchment paper overhang to lift the lemon bars out of the pan and transfer them to a cutting board.
Use a sharp knife to cut the lemon bars into squares or rectangles.
Dust the tops of the lemon bars with powdered sugar, if desired.
Serve and enjoy your delicious egg-free lemon bars!

Peanut Butter Fudge

Ingredients:

- 1 cup creamy peanut butter
- 1/2 cup unsalted dairy-free butter
- 1 teaspoon vanilla extract
- 3 cups powdered sugar
- 1/4 teaspoon salt

Instructions:

Line an 8x8-inch baking dish with parchment paper, leaving some overhang on the sides for easy removal.

In a medium saucepan, melt the peanut butter and dairy-free butter over low heat, stirring constantly.

Once melted, remove the saucepan from the heat and stir in the vanilla extract.

Gradually add the powdered sugar and salt to the peanut butter mixture, stirring until smooth and well combined. The mixture will be thick.

Pour the peanut butter fudge mixture into the prepared baking dish, spreading it out evenly with a spatula.

Place the baking dish in the refrigerator and chill the fudge for at least 2 hours, or until firm.

Once the fudge is firm, use the parchment paper overhang to lift it out of the baking dish. Use a sharp knife to cut the fudge into squares.

Serve and enjoy your delicious egg-free peanut butter fudge! Store any leftovers in an airtight container in the refrigerator.

Caramel Apple Crisp

Ingredients:

For the filling:

- 4 cups peeled and sliced apples (such as Granny Smith or Honeycrisp)
- 1/4 cup granulated sugar
- 1 tablespoon all-purpose flour
- 1/2 teaspoon ground cinnamon
- 1/4 teaspoon ground nutmeg
- 1/4 cup dairy-free caramel sauce

For the crisp topping:

- 1 cup old-fashioned oats
- 1/2 cup all-purpose flour
- 1/2 cup packed brown sugar
- 1/2 teaspoon ground cinnamon
- 1/4 teaspoon salt
- 1/2 cup unsalted dairy-free butter, melted

Instructions:

Preheat your oven to 350°F (175°C). Grease an 8x8-inch baking dish.

In a large mixing bowl, combine the sliced apples, granulated sugar, flour, cinnamon, and nutmeg. Toss until the apples are evenly coated.

Spread the apple mixture evenly into the prepared baking dish. Drizzle the dairy-free caramel sauce over the top.

In another mixing bowl, combine the oats, flour, brown sugar, cinnamon, and salt for the crisp topping.

Pour the melted dairy-free butter over the oat mixture and stir until well combined and crumbly.

Sprinkle the crisp topping evenly over the apple mixture in the baking dish.

Bake in the preheated oven for 35 to 40 minutes, or until the topping is golden brown and the apples are tender.

Remove the caramel apple crisp from the oven and let it cool for a few minutes before serving.

Serve warm, optionally with dairy-free vanilla ice cream or whipped topping.

Enjoy your delicious egg-free caramel apple crisp!

Blueberry Cobbler

Ingredients:

For the blueberry filling:

- 4 cups fresh or frozen blueberries
- 1/2 cup granulated sugar
- 2 tablespoons lemon juice
- 1 tablespoon cornstarch
- 1 teaspoon vanilla extract

For the cobbler topping:

- 1 cup all-purpose flour
- 1/4 cup granulated sugar
- 1 teaspoon baking powder
- 1/4 teaspoon salt
- 1/4 cup unsalted dairy-free butter, chilled and cubed
- 1/4 cup unsweetened almond milk (or any other plant-based milk)
- 1 teaspoon vanilla extract

Instructions:

Preheat your oven to 375°F (190°C). Grease a 9-inch square baking dish or a similar-sized dish.

In a large mixing bowl, combine the blueberries, granulated sugar, lemon juice, cornstarch, and vanilla extract. Toss until the blueberries are evenly coated, then spread them evenly in the prepared baking dish.

In another mixing bowl, whisk together the flour, granulated sugar, baking powder, and salt for the cobbler topping.

Add the chilled and cubed dairy-free butter to the flour mixture. Use a pastry cutter or your fingers to cut the butter into the flour until the mixture resembles coarse crumbs.

In a small bowl, mix together the almond milk and vanilla extract. Gradually pour the almond milk mixture into the flour mixture, stirring until a thick dough forms.

Drop spoonfuls of the cobbler topping over the blueberry filling, covering it as evenly as possible.

Bake in the preheated oven for 35 to 40 minutes, or until the cobbler topping is golden brown and the blueberry filling is bubbly.

Remove from the oven and let it cool for a few minutes before serving.

Serve warm, optionally with dairy-free vanilla ice cream or whipped topping. Enjoy your delicious egg-free blueberry cobbler!

Strawberry Rhubarb Crisp

Ingredients:

For the filling:

- 3 cups sliced fresh rhubarb
- 3 cups sliced fresh strawberries
- 1/2 cup granulated sugar
- 1/4 cup cornstarch
- 1 tablespoon lemon juice
- 1 teaspoon vanilla extract

For the crisp topping:

- 1 cup old-fashioned oats
- 1/2 cup all-purpose flour
- 1/2 cup packed brown sugar
- 1/2 teaspoon ground cinnamon
- 1/4 teaspoon salt
- 1/2 cup unsalted dairy-free butter, melted

Instructions:

Preheat your oven to 375°F (190°C). Grease an 8x8-inch baking dish.

In a large mixing bowl, combine the sliced rhubarb, sliced strawberries, granulated sugar, cornstarch, lemon juice, and vanilla extract. Toss until the fruit is evenly coated, then spread the mixture evenly in the prepared baking dish.

In another mixing bowl, combine the oats, flour, brown sugar, cinnamon, and salt for the crisp topping.

Pour the melted dairy-free butter over the oat mixture and stir until well combined and crumbly.

Sprinkle the crisp topping evenly over the fruit mixture in the baking dish.

Bake in the preheated oven for 35 to 40 minutes, or until the crisp topping is golden brown and the fruit filling is bubbling.

Remove from the oven and let it cool for a few minutes before serving.

Serve warm, optionally with dairy-free vanilla ice cream or whipped topping.

Enjoy your delicious egg-free strawberry rhubarb crisp!

Maple Pecan Pie

Ingredients:

For the crust:

- 1 1/4 cups all-purpose flour
- 1/2 cup unsalted dairy-free butter, cold and cubed
- 1/4 teaspoon salt
- 2-4 tablespoons ice water

For the filling:

- 1 cup pecan halves
- 3/4 cup maple syrup
- 1/2 cup light brown sugar
- 1/4 cup unsalted dairy-free butter, melted
- 3 tablespoons all-purpose flour
- 3 flax eggs (3 tablespoons ground flaxseed meal + 9 tablespoons water)
- 1 teaspoon vanilla extract
- 1/4 teaspoon salt

Instructions:

Preheat your oven to 375°F (190°C).

In a food processor, combine the flour and salt. Add the cold, cubed dairy-free butter and pulse until the mixture resembles coarse crumbs.

Gradually add the ice water, 1 tablespoon at a time, and pulse until the dough comes together and forms a ball.

Transfer the dough to a lightly floured surface and shape it into a disk. Wrap it in plastic wrap and refrigerate for at least 30 minutes.

Once chilled, roll out the dough on a lightly floured surface into a circle about 12 inches in diameter. Carefully transfer the dough to a 9-inch pie dish and trim any excess overhang. Crimp the edges as desired.

In a large mixing bowl, whisk together the maple syrup, brown sugar, melted dairy-free butter, flour, flax eggs, vanilla extract, and salt until well combined.

Arrange the pecan halves evenly over the bottom of the prepared pie crust.

Pour the maple syrup mixture over the pecans.

Place the pie dish on a baking sheet to catch any potential spills.

Bake in the preheated oven for 45 to 50 minutes, or until the filling is set and the crust is golden brown.

If the crust begins to brown too quickly, cover the edges with aluminum foil or a pie crust shield.

Remove the pie from the oven and let it cool completely on a wire rack before slicing and serving.
Serve your delicious egg-free maple pecan pie at room temperature or slightly warmed, optionally with dairy-free whipped cream or ice cream.
Enjoy!

Molten Lava Cake

Ingredients:

- 1/2 cup unsalted dairy-free butter
- 4 oz dairy-free semi-sweet chocolate chips
- 1/2 cup granulated sugar
- 2 flax eggs (2 tablespoons ground flaxseed meal + 6 tablespoons water)
- 2 teaspoons vanilla extract
- 1/4 cup all-purpose flour
- Pinch of salt
- Dairy-free vanilla ice cream, for serving (optional)
- Fresh berries, for garnish (optional)
- Powdered sugar, for dusting (optional)

Instructions:

Preheat your oven to 425°F (220°C). Grease four ramekins or custard cups with dairy-free butter and place them on a baking sheet.

In a microwave-safe bowl, melt the dairy-free butter and chocolate chips together in the microwave, stirring every 30 seconds until smooth. Alternatively, you can melt them together in a double boiler on the stovetop.

In a separate mixing bowl, whisk together the granulated sugar, flax eggs, and vanilla extract until well combined.

Gradually add the melted chocolate mixture to the sugar mixture, stirring until smooth.

Add the flour and salt to the chocolate mixture and stir until just combined.

Divide the batter evenly among the prepared ramekins, filling each one about 3/4 full.

Place the baking sheet with the ramekins in the preheated oven and bake for 12 to 14 minutes, or until the edges are set but the centers are still soft.

Remove the baking sheet from the oven and let the lava cakes cool for 1 to 2 minutes.

Carefully run a knife around the edges of each ramekin to loosen the cakes. Invert each cake onto a serving plate.

Serve the molten lava cakes warm, optionally topped with dairy-free vanilla ice cream, fresh berries, and a dusting of powdered sugar.

Enjoy your decadent egg-free molten lava cakes!

www.ingramcontent.com/pod-product-compliance
Lightning Source LLC
LaVergne TN
LVHW081614060526
838201LV00054B/2248